David.

Keep t
near u
up an̲d̲ ̲r̲e̲a̲d̲ ̲i̲t̲
often.

Love always
Cath.
xxxx

To my teacher Sri Kaleshwar
with love and thanks

The Song of Mother Divine

FINDHORN PRESS

Know only this:

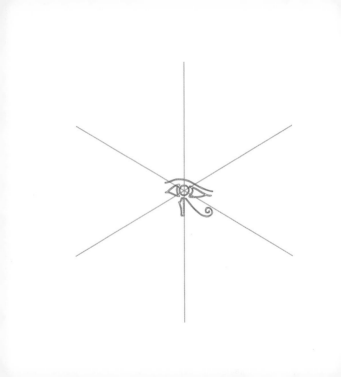

Whoever I am,
I am loved

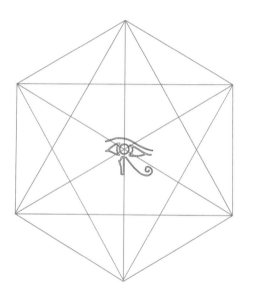

Wherever I am,
I am loved

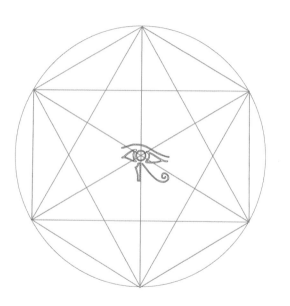

Whatever I do,
I am loved

No matter how I feel,
I am loved

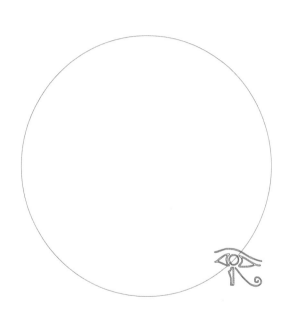

Whatever is
happening around me,
I am loved

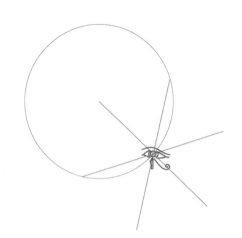

Whatever is
happening to me,
I am loved

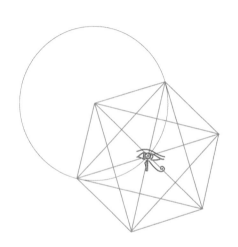

When I suffer abuse,
I am loved

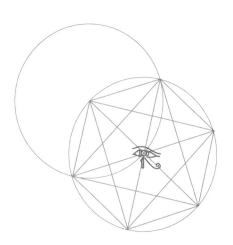

When I abuse,

I am loved

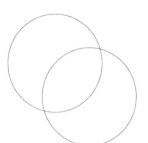

When I am angry,
I am loved

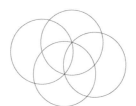

When I am at peace,
I am loved

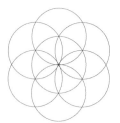

When I am afraid,
I am loved

When I am happy,
I am loved

When all
that I do is wrong,
I am loved

When no one cares,

I am loved

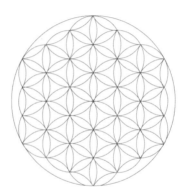

When I feel only pain,

I am loved

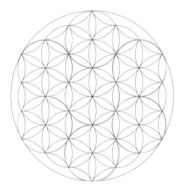

When I see only darkness,

I am loved

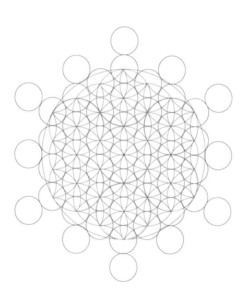

When I see only Light,
I am loved

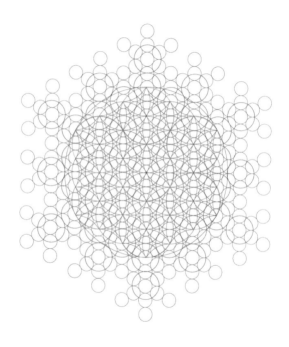

When I despair,
I am loved

When I rejoice,
I am loved

When I lay dying,

I am loved

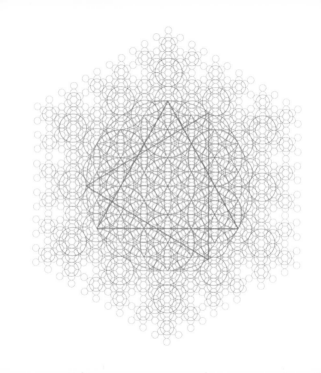

If I am desperate, poor,
cold, hungry and abandoned,
I am loved

If I am wealthy,
happy and successful,
I am loved

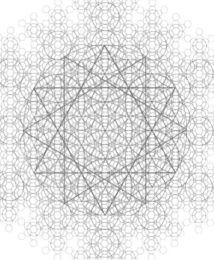

However
the world treats me,
I am loved

However
I feel about myself,
I am loved

Whoever
I believe myself to be,
I am loved

I step through
this veil of illusion now
and I know only this:

I am loved

I am loved

I am loved

I am loved

I am all that I am

So it is,

so it shall be

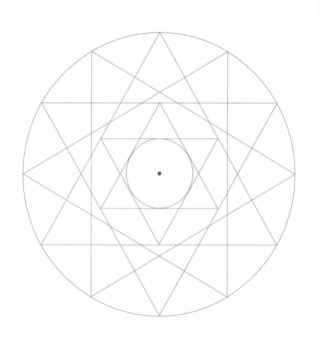

Om. Shanti. Peace.

Sue Saraswati is a teacher, healer, student and complementary therapist of great experience and ability. Sue teaches that world peace begins with inner peace and that inner peace is easier to access when mind and body are in balance. Sue acts as a catalyst to let each person find their individual path to peace, allowing their own Life Force energy to transform them into who they are. All her teaching is simple, straightforward, compassionate and full of humour!

www.suesaraswati.com

Published by Findhorn Press. All rights reserved.
Text © Sue Saraswati 2009 • Illustrations © Amy Merry 2009
ISBN 978-1-84409-149-2
Printed in China